CHARMS AGAINST LIGHTNING

JAMES ARTHUR

CHARMS AGAINST LIGHTNING

COPPER CANYON PRESS
PORT TOWNSEND, WASHINGTON

Printed in the United States of America
Cover art: Robert Motherwell, *La Mer*, Art©Dedalus Foundation, Inc./Licensed by VAGA, New York, NY

Copper Canyon Press is in residence at Fort Worden State Park in Port Townsend, Washington, under the auspices of Centrum. Centrum is a gathering place for artists and creative thinkers from around the world, students of all ages and backgrounds, and audiences seeking extraordinary cultural enrichment.

LIBRARY OF CONGRESS CATALOGING-IN-PUBLICATION DATA
Arthur, James.
Charms against lightning / James Arthur.
p. cm.
ISBN 978-1-55659-387-1 (ALK. PAPER)
I. Title.
PS3601.R7634C47 2012
811'.6—DC23
2012021558

98765432 FIRST PRINTING

COPPER CANYON PRESS

Post Office Box 271
Port Townsend, Washington 98368

www.coppercanyonpress.org

for Shannon

CONTENTS

I

II

III

IV

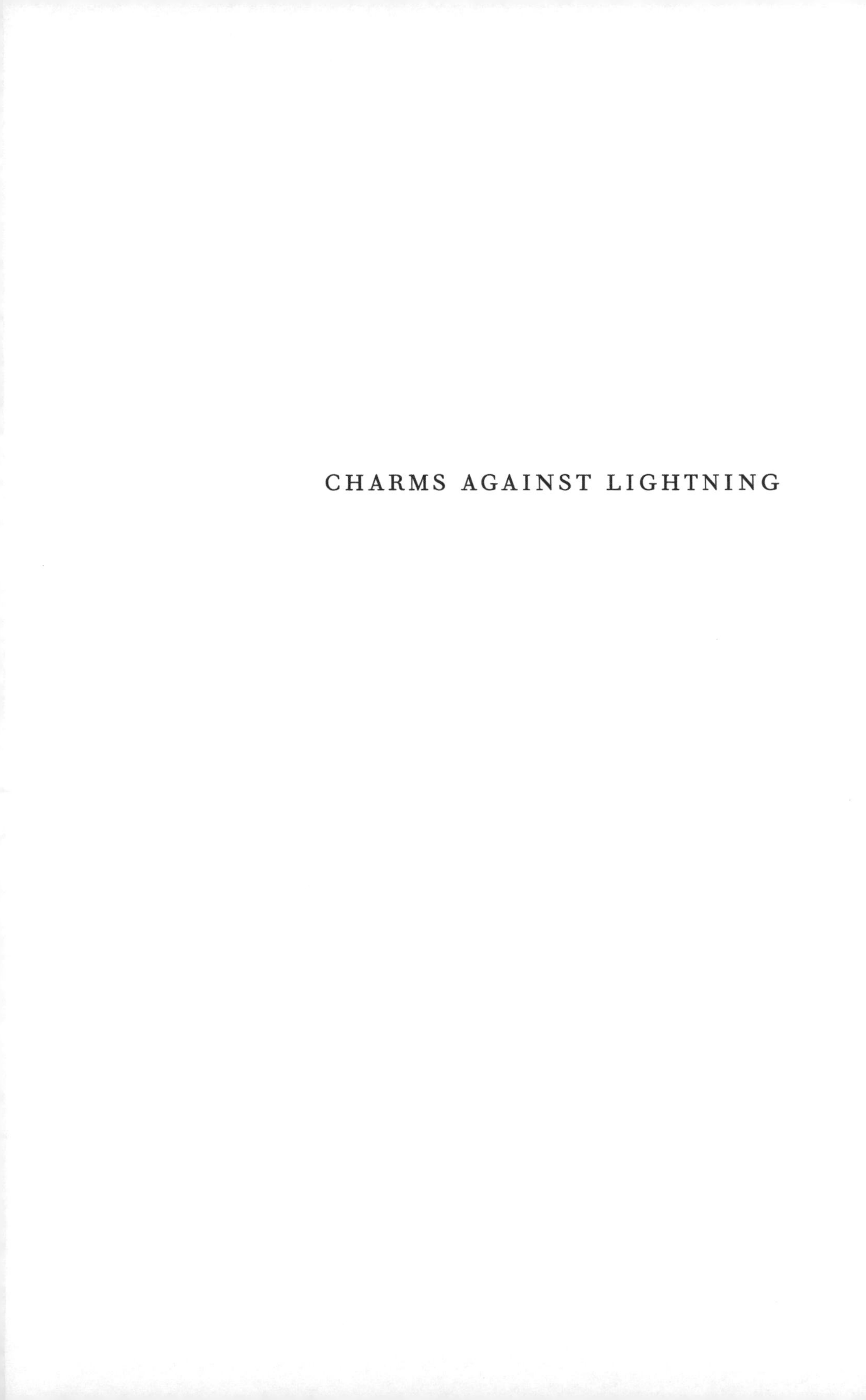

CHARMS AGAINST LIGHTNING

I

Charms Against Lightning

Against meningitis and poisoned milk,
  flash floods and heartwreck, against daydreams
Against losing your fingers, drinking detergent,
  earthquakes, baldness, divorce, against
  falling in love with a child
Against lupus and lawsuits, lying stranded between nations,
  against secrets and frostbite, the burring of trains
  that never arrive
Against songlessness, your mother's depression,
  the death of the cedars, Siberian crane
Against these talismans against lightning—
  the shutters swing, and clack their yellow teeth;
  the deep sky welters and the windows quiver

The Kitchen Weeps Onion

The kitchen weeps onion
because the cook is dead. Pans strike chorus
and the ladles keep a knock-kneed stride.
Burners gleam more brightly. *Chives,*
chives, and chives. Everyone seems so tired
but the diners can't sleep. The kitchen tonight
weeps onion, so everyone else must weep.
What's the use in talking? Let's touch,
and turn apart. The cook is quiet,
cold, unearthly, and the turnip
breaks its heart.

Ghost Life

November. My shadow steps outside, a knit scarf
double-wrapped around his throat,
wearing his feel-good canvas coat, a hand-me-down
with frayed cuffs and an ink splotch where a pen
burst in a side pocket years ago,
on a colder day. A Safeway bag blows willy-nilly

        across a puddleful of bricks...
and treetops are raucous clown wigs
and daubs of oil paint. My shadow feels my company,
my stepping as he steps, feels,
although he knows it can't be true, that the fall
and all its wreckage were invented
just for him. Nameless as a waterdrop, he walks
sideways up a wall, and is taller with every step
and thinner than a flame.

Utopia

Now he's found his own city, a postcard place
that anyone would like, backlit by the romance
of an unknown history. Here, sheets and hair
perfume the air, every gate is hammered silver,
every song, a song and dance, and the balloon seller

bares her ivory shoulder for a kiss.
The man, who's spent enormously to feed a fantasy
of being from no place—spent what he had,
and borrowed more—now is completely happy

except for an idea of an idea, which he cannot outpace,
that somehow he may have missed something
that he should not have missed, though no doubt
this is better than lying on a cold suburban beach

admiring stars so far away, he'd be seeing them
as they were before the dawn of human speech.
This is another country, not an ordinary place,
where a man, no matter how exceptional
he felt, would finally be erased.

Drying Out

Every sharp distinction cut.
I'd ride around on the bus.
I saw a fire truck in fallen flowers. So much mass
under so much nothing.
I was rattled by the sign, ELECTRIC MOTORS &
ARMATURES REWOUND.

I'd walk a mile out of my way
to not cross a bridge,
wearing wool gloves on summer days.
When touch-me-nots waved, I felt sick.

I was cold in a madrona's shadow, shocked
by the wetness of a leaf.
A shouting in the brain, awake, asleep—
I saw a lawn chair reclining in the sun
and had to shield my eyes.

Drinking Song

She and her hat came over
She crossed her legs in the sun

   her sheer hands
in the gloves they love they wear

She came over, smelling of wine
nothing of hers
being yours to accept or decline

   ————, she said
and a ship groaned in the boatyards
to the west, heard by a backhoe
its jaw to the ground

and it couldn't dig its own grave
She was all switchgrass
and began to sway, and

   ————, she said
and on came the pollen engine,
the injury machine, tocking
double-time between every tick

   Nothing of hers
being yours to accept or decline
she came over
her purse full of codeine,
and cigarettes, and twine

Vertigo

A white sail turns near Honorat
where monks murmur to their beads, and tour boats
land and leave like prying bees
since bees too turn orbits where they go,
spying into flower after flower, flying
their dizzy, hectic chores, making pollen move.
A white sail turns near Honorat
and the common gull glides by. A white sail yaws
and forever-going zephyrs confide
in the trees they shake. Waves of every size
are spat up by the sea. How should it feel
to be free? Standing in the surf
below a millstone sky, she wants to know
what moves, what is moved, by what
immense machinery…

In Praise of Noise

The sound begins with a furnace
clicking awake in a two-room house, answered
by a few, then more, voices: gauges,

and old-fashioned watches ticking out of sync, in growing number,
so their *tip-tip-tip* fattens to a moan, joined

by a horn's upbeat honkity-honk, then ringtones and speakers
rehearsing drawn horsehair, air in a woodwind, or mimicking

a hand slapping a polyester drumhead, but unlike
these coarser frictions, playing the same, every time.
A car door bangs, a jackhammer hammers, and a bassline

purrs through a wall. The sound congeals,
sucking in more, a mechanical syrup in an IV drip, the automatic

ruckus of a robotic ocean, a symphony
no one wrote, confounding every pattern:

teach me the song that no one can sing, someday
to be the song of everything.

At Klipsan Beach

The sea marks time like a sundial's arm,
steadily extending its reach.
Crawling back, it vomits on the beach—
jellyfish as violet as violets.
My whiskey, a soft amber, floating ice.

We are, and then we aren't;
that's the mortal art.

I stood dying at the ocean's side
to dream up only this.
What could I do but make my shape?
I stake my shadow to this place.

The Death of the Painter

At the end of his life
he had money and attention,
and certain towns were known
in connection to his name.

He was fastidious, and wore a tie,
was photographed with brushes, with a bird.
Under the subtropical sky
he forgave the things long done.
He hardly saw his children,
by habit was self-absorbed. His atelier
was sacrosanct, with the ocean for a view.
When he painted, it was descent
and descent and descent from the cross,
and when he died

the sepulcher was simple.
His late-life love
wept from another room.

Vertigo

beneath the sleeve
the clock face
mooning   the un-
rewinding

arms' twelve points
twelve equal
though unequal-seeming
hours   the short

hand's cycle equal
to half
the earth's own
diurnal reversal   as

if stars
were gestures   as if
by navigation   as if
a message

other than the eye
finding itself
o   i
miss you

Independence

We are famous friends, here to get drunk,
stoned, here for the fireworks,

the night of Independence Day.
Ovals spawning xeroxed ovals across a gassy sky,

each boom pursuing its fiery halo. *Happy marriage!*
someone cries. *I do, I don't,*

I might someday. Here's to the stars and bars!
To my bed, and you having nowhere else to go—

bring a kiss, not your clothes… *To the sky!*
bright as a bottle shard… To optimism,

and all the states, even the boring ones.
I know you… the skin graft on your cheek,

your lost dog, your *can't-sleep*. I might as well
be your own hand. Jesus Christ!—

take off his ring, keep it off,
and put a ring on me.

Omnivore

I eat what's put in front of me,
as all great men do. Should you eat shark? I know

some wouldn't, but I do, if it's there.
Scorpions too, and their stingers; swallowing a scorpion

won't poison you. Old-time glue-makers
made glue of old horses, and I

make use when I can.
Someone put his wife in front of me; someone else,

his mediocrity. What I know, I swear by—
feed yourself, or die.

Tyrrhenian Sea

Your eyelashes: there's
what I know about Anacapri.
And spelling out time in flashes, a lighthouse.
And the bright houses drowning
down by the sea. We swam. We drank.
We passed a bottle on the waves in the dark.

In Pompeii, which was buried by fire,
you ate smoke from my tongue.
Your skin, your skin. A cinder tree's shade;
a polyglot boy sold parasols
and there were dogs alive and dead. A three-
legged mutt turning circles: no omen,
no omen we knew. In Assisi,

where broad and shallow steps crosscut
and veered from street to street,
we feared the holy orders. At Tivoli
we leaned on a balustrade. At Frascati,
were cooled by a spigot.

Why does the tourist mind
always linger? It's no good, I know. But
you are my eyes' temple
and I've adored you where you stood.

At the Protestant Cemetery

I returned after you'd been and gone,
        saw pine trees nodding over the un-Catholic dead...
everything, as you'd say, *gone to seed—*
        you, gone back to home and husband. I found the famous poet's grave
while looking for you, found a snail
        in its own ringed tomb crawling over a headstone.
The fleshy mantle, the calcium shell.
        What kind of life
could a snail even have, tugging forward,
        towing everything behind?

On Day and Night

And as the neighbors' guests retire, coaxing their cars
into the snow (we're gazing through the curtain
into winter's pale hub), two girls gaze up. They're all
going home, like wheels correcting
into steering hands, or drawn breath returning to the air,
but you can't come back to anywhere—there's no perfect here
and there, or now and then—but here we are,
again. A silverfish crosses the windowpane. We peer
into the street, and up at the stranded moon: White wheel,
black field. Black winter, white road. White silence,
black wind. White cars, black wires.

Kiss

to inhabit as the air inhabits, coasting
invisibly through branches...
the town spreads over a gorge, houses erased by sunlight; aerials
clustering on rooftops,
blue hills receding—

"Well," you say, "we'll come back someday."

Song of the Doppelgänger

I was there, and saw the half-ton rope
of human hair coiled like a python,
glinting. I don't know when the war was fought,

why, or where it stopped, but believe
in the mighty engine perspiring behind the screen
and as much as I can
in the notion of good. I find less to praise.

I've been to the Sinai, to Kiyomizu-dera.
I went to Hiroshima and didn't cry. I know pretty well
what my promises are worth,
know the worth of material things.

Just this summer I heard a raven sing
and thought of a stone rebounding
down a bottomless jar.

In Defense of the Semicolon

> No semicolons. Semicolons indicate relationships that only idiots need defined by punctuation. RICHARD HUGO

But it's a reassuring logic that rivers freeze
because your hemisphere has rolled away from the sun,
that cities rest because there must be time for resting.
I could never deny it, or disown my desire
for the certainty of home, for mills and reservoirs
I always come back to. I'm thinking of a girl
pinning butterflies through her bangs, the first woman
I ever asked to marry me. She was slight and strange;
her brother lived in England, and was dying there.
Years after our split, she and I met in an open-air restaurant
crowded with chatter and cigarettes. I was still very young,
still afraid of being abandoned at the terminal.
She no longer ate; she had lost teeth and some hair,
she said. There were pale islands of skin
where the butterflies had perched. The waiter came around
to refill our coffee, a phone was ringing, and fifty feet away
streetcars jostled like dusk nudging against darkness;
even between those two there are gangways:
movable bridges ship-to-shore, small therefores.

Avocado

In a bowl, blind as stones.
In their soft-skinned hides, holding seeds.

Carving an avocado
makes a C-section, and the meat of the fruit
slicks the stone. My brother and I
were cut from the womb.
Our mother would have died, twice.

Happiness. You want seasons
and radio, want swallows dogfighting,
want to walk in a leather coat,
maple keys spinning down.

Fatherhood

Someday I'd like to have a daughter
and give her a stuffy name
that she'd hate. She and I
could go galumphing out to a pond
and net minnows
she'd briefly keep alive. A serious
small person, a lover of ribbons
and toboggans. Of talking, waistcoat-
wearing otters. She and I
would rake up every leaf
in November.

Am I such a sap?

Forgive me—maybe I know more
about sons. If I had one
I'd expect him
to fling any tenderness
back on my plate, to say
"You're nudging me into the grave"
when I'm telling him to live,
to not forgive, forget all
but the worst of what I say,
and magnify his victories
to win my love.

Exoskeleton

Is this armor, or your architecture?
You can't but stiffen to the touch. I wear you close and thin
and it's hunting season, so we're in orange.
Drizzle has jacketed the apple trees in silver, soaking the wheelbarrow
and its barrowful of leaves. *Tat-tat,*
scolds an assiduous woodpecker, working for a cache of bugs.
The pecked tree, wounded after all, gives what it has
to the bird, and I claim your name at every word, claim you,
who think you belong to yourself.

Vertigo

Copper geese
revolving on a weather vane, searching for a tailwind,

as if they had somewhere to go:
I know it's dumb, but I feel sad for them,
seeing them creak on their spindle.
Don't I pull you on, as if we too

were joined on a stem?
Back to someplace we've been,
or onward, to some place of promise?

I hate these verandas and gables, all this wooden siding.
I wish I could see this city
as I will years from now.

The wind picks up; the geese turn again.

Against Emptiness

Denser than a dog. Volatile
like a torpedo, harder than a punch line
and more foreseeable. Are these the days
of easy praise? A man strays through humid roses,

watching gardengoers gaze. More
than you imagine, less than he thinks, inkier
than a printmaker's fingerprints. Nothing
will come of nothing, someone once said.

The first poem I wrote, I wrote for a girl,
knowing for certain what I meant. More intertwining
than a Celtic knot. More beseeching
than a forget-me-not. More far-reaching

and daring, more engaged
with the world. Can a man build a tower
out of air alone? He can. And the wind
will blow it away.

III

In Praise of the Indeterminate

It has no form, and out-Houdinis Houdini
by dissolving from shape to shape, struggling
to escape itself, remaining the same thing,
like a video feed of the almost-random variations
in the similarity of the sea. It becomes melon-seed,

a cider press. It knows that what it sees
it sees through the pinhole of one consciousness.
It says a star is a star is a hydrogen bomb.
Like an envoy sent back from the last evolution
of the human race, it has no face

and knows more than it understands.
It says the makers of the Parthenon aren't to blame
for framing the symmetries of a rational age

when planets turned in harmonic spheres
chasing the enigmatic moon, which now we know
to be floating away from Earth forever
at the rate of an inch per year, give or take.
It defends your freedom to be wrong
and promote your point of view,

your freedom to give up your freedom
by degrees. It's the silt and the dam:
impregnable, a Sing Sing, a jukebox
grinding out the tune
that you yearn for, and can't name.

The Disconnected Man

They say the world is dying,
that we need to farm the wind. Wind harvesters

turn against a sky white as plate,
pinwheels crowning poles, spinning wind

into electricity. I see and hear
the glow and grinding: the can opener's

rasp-hum, a rush of steam, a trickle
in the coffee machine as the Pyrex pot

fills up. My boots, asleep by the upstairs door.
I want more. Am I a man on a column

going crazy or blind? The phone rings.
No caller, only dial tone—

Bucephalus, Charging

Riding over Persia
on titanium hooves, my gallop
tearing up the DMZ,

I stomp down a refinery, trail a scat
of incinerated cars, running
from my shadow

as I strike at the sun. One brown eye,
one blue. I'm star-marked...
my barding, bulletproof.

I'm the noise of a wedding
on fire. Bombed-out tenements
quake as I pass. In my blinders

and heavy headstall, I smell
petroleum burning and hear
a high-winding cry.

In a Parallel Universe

"I mean, *back in the day,*" said The Face, meaning
before he was born: when no one carried a phone
but people had them at home. Or before then—

pre-Kennedy, pre-Nixon—when streetcars
were unknown, and men whose sons
would storm foxholes in World War I

spent so much time standing around, smoking.
To go far away, you went by boat or train
and the "near" of today *was* far away, and you died

in the town you were born in. He said, "I'm not saying
things were better back then."
As well as he knew anything, he knew, as long

as there's been a then and a now, there's been
someone to say the world was better *back when*...
"And *I* am not saying so," said The Face, "I know

there never was any Eden. But back in the day
if word had come down of Neil Armstrong
landing on the moon, it would never

have crossed your mind that the whole thing—
the small step, a leap for mankind—was a lie
filmed on a subterranean sound stage."

Poem from Behind a Gorilla Mask

Fuck you to the following:
(I can’t keep track of names) anyone you know
with a waterfront view. All your accusers
and all whom they accuse. The many aching
to be the few. Drum-bangers, gangbangers,
self-hangers, demigods. Those who make the love,
love the peace, or make the killing.
I include myself as well; I know how sympathy
rots the heart. Thank you
for your love. You get my pity in return.
I wrote this on a Tuesday
sitting in the park.

Disintegration

Take me down to Shitcan City—
    show me your famous graffiti on a famous wall.
Out in sour sulk rains.

    What do you mean, "satisfied"?
Show me your lasting peace, and the logo on your thigh.

    In your translucent studio
we'll hear nighttime braying in the petting zoo. I went
to buy a BeoCom

and came back with a mind full of bric-a-brac.
            I went to get her poor dog a bone.

Take me down
    to the water plant in the evening.
Dress me up in riot gear—send me off,

sell me piecemeal, write a letter to my widow,
    sign it with a signing machine.

The Sympathy of Angels

Being of tragic bent
we incline to the future

and the past. But we
see you. We
see how tired you are
as you lean on your rifle

or your shovel.
We see the fired shells
and the head they go into.
We too are shells,
you too are graves.
Equally to all men, we

have nothing to say.
Adore. We are just. We
serve a monarch
in a silk sarcophagus.

Sad Robots

clean steel: inflexible, but
where they're strong

is where they're weak. ginsu knives,
not flesh, they cut themselves, and fall apart.

what do they want?
to be waterfalls or to give new leaf

to bend, unclench
to grow a peach

Oysterville

Beside your trinket house
the garden gathered rain. I pulled pears
from the pear tree, and saw a few things
grow (the wise, dumb pumpkins
engorged below the gate…).
I split a stump, wrote letters, gathered
oysters, ate the rain.

Reed Ships

All colliding bodies
should collide somewhere perpetually, and Jericho
should always be breaking,

        echoing on (reed ships
on the Tigris, hooves in the Rubicon, all circles
lapping, boat to boat)—

        Why can't I remember
what everyone knows?
No utterance endures. Air carries sound.
No voice leaves the Earth
unless it leaves as light.

The Names of Flowers

Baby's breath. Black-eyed Susan. Do you take
these things named after us—

this carnation, grown of carnality,
pledged at its root to the flesh?

Where is the groomsman headed,
with what address written on his hand?

It's you on display in the basket;
the body all ablush must come out.

The wedding's a near cry from a wake.

Whatever you were vowing, vow again.
The roar in the garden is the grave.

Aspirations

after W.H. Auden

to address mystery
without being mysterious,
never expecting anyone
to know, speaking only for yourself

but not being self-centered,
conducting yourself
as if your work matters, knowing nothing

makes nothing happen, never naming
what you love, believing in truth—
as who doesn't?—and not selling
something, not contenting yourself

with saying nothing, to bow down
and obey, *to hate nothing*
and to ask nothing for its love

Sprezzatura

Effortlessness, I learn again,
means putting all opinion & mulishness aside,

so when this almost-nothingness
alights, as occasionally it must,
it lands with the padding footfall of a child ballerina

who's terrified to be there, & hopeful,
so that when it turns,
fast, spinning
as a dreidel spins, it seems to have no contours
or definite sides,

so that it's compact
& can deflect any point

& springs like laughter, for it's of the world
& there is such a thing

Gooseberry

Is there something you were hoping to say
now perched on your tongue
like a tern on an orca's back?

To you, dear you, these private words…
I mean, these clashing birds.
Gooseberry umbrellas have tumbled into the eyes
of the children crossing the yard.

Who thinks of these mismatched flocks,
of these thoughts that won't align?
A sleeper adrift in his chair?
Is the reading light still burning?

IV

The Land of Nod

Growing up, I barely knew the Bible, but read
and reread the part when Cain drifted east
or was drawn that way, into a place of desolation,
the land of Nod, there to begin, with a wife

of unknown origin, another race of men,
under the mark of God. As a boy, I thought Nod
would be a place where the blue scilla
would bloom gray, a country of the rack and screw,

the serrated sword, where the very serving cups
were bone. As a grown man, I've heard that Nod
never was a nation—of Cain's offspring, or anyone—
but a mistranslation of "wander," so Cain

could go wherever, and be in Nod. Far more
than in God, I believe in Cain, who destroyed
his own brother, and therefore in any city
could have his wish, and be alone.

Distracted by an Ergonomic Bicycle

On a rainy morning in the worst year
of my life, as icy eyelets shelled the street,
I shared a tremor with a Doberman
leashed to a post. We two were all the world
until a bicyclist shot by, riding

like a backward birth, feetfirst,
in level, gentle ease, with the season's hard breath
between his teeth. The rain was almost ice, the sky
mild and pale. I saw a milk carton bobbing by
on a stream of melting sleet.

A bicyclist. A bicyclist. He rode away—
to his home, I guess. I went home,
where I undressed, left my jacket
where it fell, went straight to bed, and slept
for two days straight. But those clicking wheels

kept clicking in my head, and though
I can't say why, I felt not only *not myself*
but that I'd never been... that I

was that man I hardly saw, hurling myself
into the blast, and that everything
I passed—dog, rain, cold, the other guy—
I left in my wake, like afterbirth.

Swimming Pool

A teapot, a peacoat, a butter boat.
Can you prepare for love? The stars
hole up in their blue night sleeve
and will be your dear companions
if you tell them what they are.

                    Afraid of dying,
he went for a swim: him to swim,
no one else, but never mind—
aqua-beetles made merry, and the pine stand
stood. Weed clouds wandered. *Float...*

he did. And the sprung floss of clouds
spun darker. The air shot wet. Unfelt touches
set the swimming pool atilt. *Rain.*
Lip to lip, it's inert, but what a lot
a lot can do. The pool cried, *Are they done,*
your days of glass?

A sky, a frown, a sky-blue surface
pelted down
with leaping tin. Let fall! Let spring!
He wasn't struck by lightning—

Daylight Savings

Give me some light
in the maplefire, in the sudden fierce embranglement

        and rapid setting on
of this wind, its sweep that bends the saplings
and deforms the standing leaves.
I rewind the hour hand… evening takes over
the road. A bus making headway
on a splashing lane; its taillights

smear and bend. I drank all I could, couldn't die,
now I'm here alive.
I'll take all the day I can find, and dig,
and crack stone till it gives ore.

You Are the Canal Dividing a City

You are the canal dividing a city
        where the winter is too warm
to freeze you. You transport salt water
                into fresh, and ships to the sea. Counterweights
lift your bridges. You've kept your course,
                        filling and pouring. You travel
and don't depart. You'd carry a body
                as you would any thing. You have no mind
but for miles, you touch, and all day
        people stop and look at you.

Epithalamium

I will be very sorry
for all the things that I do
as long as we both shall live
and you will tell me
until you've convinced yourself
that there is nothing
to forgive.

Rapid Transit

One train overtakes another going the same way,
so two sets of passengers come eye-to-eye

and out one side of each train
a world flashes by, and opposite,
a world of strangers, passing slow.
As one end of a kayaker's paddle cuts into a lake

the other end flings water at the sky.
A hand that can squeeze into a fist, turn a key,
or stroke her cheek is the perfect, backward twin
of the other, clumsy one.
Somewhere it's early evening, but here, early morning:

into a smack of yawning air, the overtaking train
snaps free. Sunflash, stereo store,
a boy bends down, seeing a nickel—

Tropical Bats

Numberless, from a cleft in the mountainside
at last light, flying close above the cane field—

over you, me, a few trees, and snapped-off palm fronds—
flying noisier than rain, in zigzag. One wing's
pat-pat, caught somehow and magnified,

echoes down to us. As whirring fills the air, we start naming things
to which we can compare this yarn of sound
and the shape of the bats' many-bodied wave—

their tribe, their line, their sudden veer. A hawk circles
high and wide. There must've been a time
no history records, when cavemen, seeing

a phenomenon they'd never seen, would've been held
in undescribing awe.

An outcry is what I mean, what this flock reminds me of—
a voice declaring, if only to the air, its drive
to keep alive, longer, and ferociously.

Summer Song

Fifty floors above the street,
you in a summer dress. Star-shaped holes in a steel chandelier
giving shape to the stars' elsewhereness—

Or a tall flag snaps
against a sour-looking sky, and troopers sailing in by parachute
are clothespins
pinning up the sky. Or someone sets a fire

by kissing an inlaid floor of stone.
In the subway, we see an old woman
a million miles from home. The galaxies known by number
outnumbering those with names…
I marry you in the morning
and I marry you each day.

I feel the strain inside the song,
the Atlantic in the shell.
I feel a tall wind rising up to take
and bear me far away.

ABOUT THE AUTHOR

James Arthur was born in Connecticut and grew up in Toronto, Canada. He has received a Stegner Fellowship, a Hodder Fellowship, the Amy Lowell Poetry Travelling Scholarship, a Discovery/The Nation Prize, and a residency at the Amy Clampitt House, as well as fellowships at Yaddo and the MacDowell Colony. He did his graduate work at the University of Washington in Seattle and at the University of New Brunswick in Fredericton. He now lives in Princeton, New Jersey, with his wife and son.

ACKNOWLEDGMENTS

Grateful acknowledgment is made to the editors of the books and periodicals in which versions these poems first appeared:

32 Poems: "Against Emptiness," "The Sympathy of Angels"; *AGNI Online:* "Drying Out," "The Kitchen Weeps Onion," "Poem from Behind a Gorilla Mask"; *The American Poetry Review*: "In A Parallel Universe," "Sprezzatura," "Tropical Bats"; *The Antioch Review:* "Exoskeleton"; *Best New Poets 2010:* "Independence"; *Brick:* "Distracted by an Ergonomic Bicycle," "In Defense of the Semicolon," "Tyrrhenian Sea"; *Cranky:* "At Klipsan Beach," "Reed Ships"; *The Fiddlehead:* "You Are the Canal Dividing a City"; *Fox Chase Review:* "Bucephalus, Charging"; *The Laurel Review:* "Swimming Pool"; *Literary Review of Canada:* "The Disconnected Man," "Oysterville"; *Many Mountains Moving:* "Charms Against Lightning"; *Narrative:* "Drinking Song," "Epithalamium," "Ghost Life," "Kiss," "Omnivore," "Rapid Transit," "Song of the Doppelgänger," "Summer Song," "Vertigo" (Copper geese); *New England Review:* "In Praise of the Indeterminate," "Utopia"; *The New Republic:* "On Day and Night"; *The New Yorker:* "The Death of the Painter"; *Ploughshares:* "Aspirations"; *Poetry:* "The Land of Nod"; *Poetry International:* "Daylight Savings," "Fatherhood"; *Puerto del Sol:* "At the Protestant Cemetery"; *Rattle:* "Sad Robots"; *Shenandoah:* "In Praise of Noise," "The Names of Flowers," "Vertigo" (A white sail turns near Honorat); *Third Coast:* "Avocado," "Vertigo" (beneath the sleeve).

"On Day and Night" was also published on *Verse Daily.* "Tyrrhenian Sea" was reprinted in *The Best Canadian Poetry in English of 2008* (Tightrope Books, 2008), "The Names of Flowers" in *GULCH* (Tightrope Books, 2009), and "In Defense of the Semicolon" in *Breathe: 101 Contemporary Odes* (C&R Press, 2009). Some of the poems appeared in *Song of the Species,* a chapbook published in 2010 by Finishing Line Press. "Charms Against Lightning" was republished in 2012 as a "Finding" in *Geist*. "Omnivore" was reprinted in 2012 by Broadsided Press.

I could not have written these poems without the generous support of the Amy Lowell Trust, the Anderson Center for Interdisciplinary Studies, the Bread Loaf Writers' Conference, the Canada Council for the Arts, the Corporation of Yaddo, the Espy Foundation, the Kimmel Harding Nelson Center for the Arts, La Napoule Art Foundation, the MacDowell Colony, the Ontario Arts Council, the Richard Hugo House, the Sewanee Writers' Conference, Spiro Arts, the Stanford Creative Writing Program, the University of Washington Creative Writing Program, and the Unterberg Poetry Center.

I'm very grateful to the friends and teachers who read these poems—Tim Ackerman, Deni Béchard, Linda Bierds, Eavan Boland, W.S. Di Piero, Ken Fields, Rick Kenney, Ross Leckie, Colleen McElroy, Heather McHugh, Richard Newman, and also my brilliant classmates at the University of Washington and Stanford. Patrick Donnelly's insights gave shape and direction to this book.

Thank you a thousand times to Michael Wiegers and everyone at Copper Canyon Press for giving these poems a home in print.

I'm sustained by my wife, Shannon, and by the rest of my family; their love anchors me. For that, I'm more grateful than I can say.

Lannan Literary Selections

For two decades Lannan Foundation has supported the publication and distribution of exceptional literary works. Copper Canyon Press gratefully acknowledges their support.

LANNAN LITERARY SELECTIONS 2012

Matthew Dickman and Michael Dickman, *50 American Plays*

Michael McGriff, *Home Burial*

Tung Hui-Hu, *Greenhouses, Lighthouses*

James Arthur, *Charms Against Lightning*

Natalie Diaz, *When My Brother Was an Aztec*

RECENT LANNAN LITERARY SELECTIONS FROM COPPER CANYON PRESS

Michael Dickman, *Flies*

Laura Kasischke, *Space, In Chains*

Deborah Landau, *The Last Usable Hour*

Sarah Lindsay, *Twigs and Knucklebones*

Heather McHugh, *Upgraded to Serious*

W.S. Merwin, *Migration: New & Selected Poems*

Valzhyna Mort, *Collected Body*

Taha Muhammad Ali, *So What: New & Selected Poems, 1971-2005*, translated by Peter Cole, Yahya Hijazi, and Gabriel Levin

Lucia Perillo, *Inseminating the Elephant*

Ruth Stone, *In the Next Galaxy*

John Taggart, *Is Music: Selected Poems*

Jean Valentine, *Break the Glass*

C.D. Wright, *One Big Self: An Investigation*

Dean Young, *Fall Higher*

For a complete list of Lannan Literary Selections from Copper Canyon Press, please visit Partners on our Web site: www.coppercanyonpress.org

Since 1972, Copper Canyon Press has fostered the work of emerging, established, and world-renowned poets for an expanding audience. The Press thrives with the generous patronage of readers, writers, booksellers, librarians, teachers, students, and funders—everyone who shares the belief that poetry is vital to language and living.

MAJOR SUPPORT HAS BEEN PROVIDED BY:

THE PAUL G. ALLEN FAMILY FOUNDATION

amazon.com

Lannan

The Paul G. Allen Family Foundation
Amazon.com
Anonymous
Arcadia Fund
John Branch
Diana and Jay Broze
Beroz Ferrell & The Point, LLC
Mimi Gardner Gates
Golden Lasso, LLC
Gull Industries, Inc.
on behalf of William and Ruth True
Carolyn and Robert Hedin
Lannan Foundation
Rhoady and Jeanne Marie Lee
Maureen Lee and Mark Busto
The Maurer Family Foundation
National Endowment for the Arts
New Mexico Community Foundation
H. Stewart Parker
Penny and Jerry Peabody
Joseph C. Roberts
Cynthia Lovelace Sears and Frank Buxton
The Seattle Foundation
Washington State Arts Commission
Charles and Barbara Wright
The dedicated interns and faithful
volunteers of Copper Canyon Press

To learn more about underwriting Copper Canyon Press titles,
please call 360-385-4925 ext. 103

The poems are set in Fournier.
Book design and composition by Phil Kovacevich. Printed on
archival-quality paper at McNaughton & Gunn, Inc.

The Chinese character for poetry is made up of two parts:
"word" and "temple." It also serves as pressmark for
Copper Canyon Press.